da nello
RESTAURANT

4/8/09

To John
Buon Appétit

from your favourite
Restaurant in Guernsey

PUBLISHED BY

da nello
RESTAURANT

46 Lower Pollet
St Peter Port
Guernsey
GY1 1WF
Tel +44 (0)1481 721552
email: danello@cwgsy.net

ISBN (10) 1-905385-16-1
(13) 978-1-905385-16-4

First published 2006
copyright © text da nello
copyright © pictures Chris Andrews
Produced for da nello by Chris Andrews
Publications, Oxford and Channel Islands.
www.cap–ox.co.uk
Printed by Butler and Tanner, Frome

RECIPES FROM

da nello
RESTAURANT

ONLY IN
GUERNSEY

RECIPES FROM DA NELLO
RESTAURANT

A celebration of twenty eight years of good food in the
charming Island of Guernsey

CONTENTS

INTRODUCTION

When Chris Andrews suggested a Da Nello cookbook, I was right there. Then came second thoughts. After all, when bookshops and prime-time TV are crammed full of charismatic super-chefs whipping up groundbreaking dishes, what could a busy, long running, Italian restaurant possibly offer the home cook?

But, as the idea grew, we knew it made sense. After all, home is where most of us eat most of our meals most of the time and the first commandment of Italian cooking is that food must fit the daily round. The domestic kitchen is a place for dishes that are simple, fresh, satisfying and wholesome, that can be created and enjoyed day after day and still leave time for children, laughter, arguments, football, flirting and all those other things that make the world go round. Twenty eight years on, the Da Nello menu has grown into just that: a practical blend of Italian food-culture and good quality, seasonal ingredients, sourced either locally or from as close to home as possible, cooked simply but with passion.

That may not be revolutionary, but this book was never intended to be a culinary trailblazer. Whilst many of the recipes are our own, inspiration for others came from eating experiences in venues like Venice, Hong Kong, Rome and Biarritz. Recipes make it into Tim Vidamour's kitchen, onto Da Nello's tables and, finally, into this book for one simple reason: people enjoy eating them time and again. That principle has built a loyal and diverse following and that, for me, is the best accolade of all.

So here they are: Da Nello's favourite recipes, without Michelin stars, hard-to-buy ingredients or complex sauces and, believe me, no sign of a TV series either. Just dishes that we love to cook, serve and eat – day after day. We hope that you will too; and still have time for all that other good stuff.

Buon appetito!

Nello Ciotti

NUMBER 46 ... THE HISTORY

With first records of a harbour dating from 1060, Guernsey's capital carries her age well. St Peter Port's skyline is a throng of old stone buildings that seem to climb over each other to welcome seafarers. Le Pollet winds through the old town's historic heart; a busy street studded with restaurants, bars and small boutiques. It is here, at number 46, that a new Italian restaurant opened for the first time on 22nd June 1978.

With its Latin pedigree, Da Nello was in good company. Traces of Guernsey's Roman occupation lurked deep within the building's foundations and, close by, evidence of wine, oil and garum – the Empire's favourite fish sauce – was unearthed during the discovery of a waterside trading station dating from the 3rd century A.D.

Number 46 remains the oldest surviving structure in the area and a history lesson in its own right. Dating from around 1450, the two-storey building was originally known as La Tourgand: St Peter Port's northernmost defensive gate. Travellers landed at the nearby White Rock by boat, probably pausing to give thanks for safe passage at the Chapel of St Julian, which stood near the site of today's square rig mast. Their relief on passing through La Tourgand is echoed in the banter of today's visiting yachtsmen, celebrating a safe landfall on the very same spot. A colossal fireplace (now housing the bar) is evidence of the building's status. Forming part of the stone hood, a rare stone bracket would once have sported statues of saints or the Monarch of the day, probably Henry VI. The building's frontage was remixed some 300 years later as a colourful palette of blue and pink Guernsey granites, with splashes of red Alderney and white Portland stones.

The 19th century brought many changes, as number 46 was transformed first into a hotel and then a bakery before becoming Stainer's Restaurant, a green grocers, a general store, Deane's Coffee Shop, Steak House La Belle Epoque and, finally, Da Nello Restaurant.

A steady stream of rebuilds rethinks and makeovers during the next quarter century have combined to create a cosy, welcoming labyrinth which, even to regulars, seems much too big to fit inside number 46.

Da Nello is now Guernsey's longest running owner-run restaurant. In spite of changing tastes and food-fashions, it counts customers of all ages and nationalities amongst its regulars.

Such wide and enduring appeal makes it difficult to pigeonhole Da Nello. Its spirit is proudly Italian whilst the buzz is pure Guernsey. Restaurants come and go, but – like number 46 – Da Nello goes on evolving and maturing, year after year. Rome, don't forget, wasn't built in a day.

GUERNSEY – AN ISLAND OF PLENTY

On the face of it, Guernsey's big-city concentration of restaurants, bars and cafés is striking. But look a little closer and it's easy to see why islanders take food so seriously. Norman roots and a cosmopolitan, seafaring heritage combine with an idyllic horticultural climate, bountiful ocean and probably the world's best milk to make this the perfect place for eating and drinking.

So, what's on offer? Plenty, including an abundance of fresh, world-class seafood. Fish has long been the local staple and a valuable source of income. Preserved by salting or drying, it was the islands' main export throughout the Middle Ages. *Saleries* (salting places) and *Eperqueries* (drying places) were built around the Bailiwick's coastline, to preserve conger eel and mackerel. Sailing ships arrived laden with wine from Gascony, often returning home bearing valuable cargoes of salted Guernsey fish.

Today, the bulk of the daily catch is delivered direct to France, but Guernsey boats still bring home plenty. Favourites include turbot – a magnificent flat fish, traditionally cooked in a kettle – as well as brill, bass, monkfish and Dover sole. Shellfish stars include scallops, chancre (crab) and oysters, plus magnificent lobsters, whose taste and texture are a world away from low cost, air-freighted rivals.

Locals may share a deep affection for their cows; but they are not the only ones. The Guernsey breed traces its roots back to old Normandy and is now well established throughout North America and Australia, where its rich, creamy milk is a firm favourite. The secret lies not in their gentle nature, but in their stomachs: Guernseys don't digest carotene as other breeds do, which accounts for their sunny, golden milk, cream and butter. For local chefs that means authentic Norman dishes and some dangerously delicious desserts.

Guernsey beef is instantly recognisable for its distinctive yellow fat, which lends the meat a fulsome, old-fashioned flavour. Formerly seen as merely a by-product of the dairy industry, Guernsey beef is now fêted by top TV celebrity chefs, who have championed the breed's healthy pedigree and natural, wholesome taste.

Guernsey's bright, clear light has drawn generations of artists to the islands, including Renoir and William Caparne. That same sunlight sustains a healthy horticultural industry that once fed mainland Britain with mouth-watering melons, gorgeous grapes and, of course, the famous Guernsey tomatoes. Although much slimmed down, the industry still produces outstanding vegetables, herbs and fruit, which locals traditionally shop for at roadside stalls; affectionately known as 'hedge veg'.

Local brewing is thriving, but that's not all: once a central pillar of the Bailiwick's Norman character, cider production has returned to Guernsey, with shady orchards once more spreading across sleepy, rural valleys.

Sark is celebrated for its lamb, reared on the island's salt-soaked cliff top meadows, or côtils. The animals are not only known for their unique flavour, but also for their turn of speed: racing fans will relish Sark's offbeat, annual sheep racing meeting.

Even pig rearing is starting to raise its snout again, with traditional, rare breeds seen rooting through the islands' pastures once more.

All in all, Guernsey and her islands have something to satisfy the most discerning palate. Whatever your taste you certainly won't go hungry in this, the most Epicurean of archipelagoes.

THE MAKING OF A RESTAURANT

What makes a good restaurant? Great food, surely? If only it was that simple. 'Atmosphere' is probably nearer the truth: that elusive blend of style, décor, attitude, position, space, service, clientele and, yes, cuisine. Plus a big, fat pinch of luck.

Ask me what's the vital quality needed to run a restaurant and the answer is much easier: you must like people. In Italy, talking, relaxing and eating well together are not just part of life – they are the glue that holds life together. After more than 45 years in catering I am convinced that no nation is any different and that, given half a chance, most people would happily pass their time in exactly the same way. Dare I say it? Deep down we are all Italians.

I think it's that love of people that has shaped my career in a game that breaks at least as many players as it makes. From my earliest childhood memories in the mountains of central Italy, I have always enjoyed chatting to people. Like the German soldier in wartime L'Aquila, who must have marvelled at the cheek of the little boy who demanded to buy his horse. Despite some hard bargaining I didn't close the deal. But I did raise a smile, share a laugh and probably remind him of home.

My family – with my five older sisters – moved down into the heat of Rome when I was seven years old. Four years later I was sent north to a catering school in Montecatini, near Florence, where I started learning to be a chef. It was a great opportunity but I knew it wasn't for me; I wanted to be the other side of those swing doors. I wanted to meet people

After some work experience in Italy and France I was ready to join the wave of young Italians that was rolling across Europe. It took a few of us to the shores of a small British island resort, off the cost of Normandy, which I had never even heard of. Some worked for a season and moved on, but, despite the strange food, warm beer and unpredictable weather, I found that I actually liked the place. Life in Guernsey in 1958 was easy, with plenty of work and lots of fun. Places like the Channel Hotel, St George's Hall and the Normandy Beer Garden seemed to be packed full of people every night, hell bent on enjoying themselves.

I met and married Della Brehaut, a local girl from St Martin's, and settled into island life. After a short spell as cabin crew on Alitalia I worked in establishments like The Grove, on the High Street, The Shamrock (later The Morocco, close to Da Nello), the Hotel de Havelet, La Fregate, The Atlantique and, finally, for six years at the Royal Hotel, as Restaurant Manager. Along the way we bought our first house, raised a son, Marco, and I learned a lot from some superb bosses. We also paid regular visits to Italy, where Fred, my ever-practical father-in-law, came to terms with pasta and conversed with my family in Guernsey French.

By 1978 I was ready to go out on my own, so we opened Da Nello (which translates as 'Nello's') at 46 Le Pollet. It was hard but we soon realised that we could make it work. The following year I employed a local teenager who had deputised for my Italian Head Chef while he dozed in the corner. That youngster had potential, but no one could have foreseen just how much. Tim Vidamour is a big part of the Da Nello story and, 27 years later, he is still smiling and calmly feeding over 100 people most nights.

Manuel Teixeira joined us as Restaurant Manager and, together they helped Della and me to take Da Nello through many major and minor alterations, to create the thriving business that it is today.

No sane person could ever claim that running a restaurant is easy; but that is not to say that there are no laughs along the way. I have had plenty, including a lively encounter with Guernsey's late, celebrated, international arm wrestling thespian, Oliver Reed. Unaccompanied by his usual drinking chum on this occasion, he challenged me to a bout of arm wrestling. I accepted and he won easily, of course, but I let slip that I knew a man who could probably beat him. The actor's eyes lit up and he demanded that I bring him to the table immediately. I pointed out that this was impossible: Fulvio, a school friend, barman and Italian national gymnast, was in Rome. Reed grinned, drained his glass, reached into his pocket and produced a big wallet:

'OK, you and me are flying to Rome. Now.'

He meant it and the more I laughed, waffled and made excuses, the more he taunted me. Maybe I should have done it.

Some regular customers ask me when I plan to 'take it easy'. The fact is that I still love what I do and manage to combine it with plenty of time aboard our boat, exploring the islands and neighbouring French coast.

Retire? Come on; where else am I going to have this much fun on a Friday night? You tell me?

Nello Ciotti

A DAY IN THE LIFE ... 9.30 a.m.

The chef de partie shivers and unlocks the front door of Da Nello, recalling the warmth of March in his native Madeira. He blows on his hands before starting the shuttle between bar and kitchen, ferrying the daily mountain of fresh vegetables, milk, meat and bread that were delivered in the darkness. All this will fuel Da Nello's hungry kitchen for one more day. He nods a greeting to the proprietor, who is already in conclave with the head chef and restaurant manager in the back room, known as the saletta, hammering and scribbling out next quarter's menu.

A Latvian chef de partie and a French waiter join in to form a silent column of worker ants. The sleeping restaurant is in darkness, with only white tablecloths and shining cutlery to lighten its many corners.

The kitchen is a battleship's turret: all steel edges, hot metal and secret cubby-holes that must be crammed with ammunition each time it goes into action. Now it's silent. An apprentice arrives, cocooned in headphones, with a commis who tackles the bags of veg, showering soil on gleaming stainless steel.

'Bonjour', 'Hi', 'Bon dia' and then back to the usual banter: football, home, girls and football. Outside, the first batch of coffee bubbles at the waiters' station. The Frenchman is munching something flaky in a paper bag, from the boulangerie opposite. He sprays crumbs, assuring a big Slovakian waiter that fresh croissant is the ultimate *petit déjeuner*. The spiky-haired Slav rubs his eyes, shakes his head and pours himself a chipped Arsenal mug of steaming black coffee.

Things move up a gear with the arrival of the sous chef, chin buried deep in his bulky ski-jacket. He peels off the coat, unveiling the cheeky smirk that will carry him through another long day, and goes straight into checking the deliveries. The kitchen hands pick up the pace, doors swinging and pots banging.

The bar is waking up. The headwaiter press-gangs the dishwasher into helping him carry out the two leaden, hook-on window boxes full of flowers. Armed with brush and soapy bucket, a waitress attacks Da Nello's stretch of pavement. The postman darts in with a bulging bundle of brown bills, sneaking a rear view of her low-cut jeans as he skips over the steaming suds.

Within the next hour toilets will be scrubbed, vegetables peeled, sauces mixed, floors swept, fish cleaned and light bulbs replaced. The bar will welcome wishful sales reps and two wine deliverymen, who will sip cappucino, jab fingers and philosophise over last night's match. It's another day.

THE RECIPES
LE RICETTE

STARTERS

Primi Piatti

20   Fish soup – *Brodetto di pesce*

22   Duo of spinach and roasted pepper soup – *Zuppa di spinaci e peperoni arrosto*

24   Tris of Guernsey crab – *Tris di granchio*

26   Dry fried scallops gremolata – *Cappesante alla gremolata*

28   Warm canon of lamb with roasted pepper salad and anchovy cream – *Agnello con peperoni e crema d'acciughe*

32   Roasted sweet balsamic onions – *Cipolle balsamico agro-dolce*

34   Carpaccio of beef with rocket lettuce and flakes of Parmesan – *Carpaccio di manzo con rucola e Parmigiano*

36   Linguine lobster – *Linguine all'astaco*

38   Crab thermidor – *Granchio thermidor*

40   Vermicelli with oysters in Champagne sauce – *Vermicelli con ostriche e Champagne*

Fish Soup

Brodetto di Pesce

SERVES FOUR PEOPLE

Ingredients

1½ ltr of fish stock – home made is best for this (see page 110)

1 onion, finely chopped

2 carrots, chopped to 1½ cm pieces

1 celery stick, chopped to 1½ cm pieces

1 leek, chopped to 1½ cm pieces

2 medium tomatoes (peeled, de-seeded and chopped up)

4 lovage leaves, thinly sliced. If you don't have any you can use celery leaves

1 tsp chopped parsley

1 tsp ground cumin

12 mussels

4 scallops, sliced in half across

8 raw prawn tails, sliced lengthways in half

200g fresh squid, thinly sliced

200g firm white fish (e.g. brill, turbot or monkfish), cut into 2cm cubes

Method

1   Bring the prepared fish stock to the boil and then lower to a simmer. Add the chopped vegetables, except tomatoes, and simmer for 5–6 minutes.

2   Next, add the tomatoes, cumin, parsley and lovage leaves. Bring back to a simmer and then add the fish; firmer ones first i.e. monkfish, squid, prawn tails and then scallops. Bring to boil and add the mussels.

3   Simmer for 3–5 minutes or until the fish and vegetables are cooked. Divide equally into fish bowls and serve with crusty garlic bread.

"One of my best customers used to call this 'fishestrone'. It is a classic Italian fish soup. The more generous you are with the fish, the better it works. In fact ours is nearer to a fish stew and a larger version, served with crusty bread, makes an excellent main course."

NELLO CIOTTI

Duo of spinach and roasted pepper soup

Zuppa di spinaci e peperoni arrosto

SERVES SIX PEOPLE

Ingredients

Roasted pepper soup

2 cloves of garlic, chopped

2 red peppers, roasted, peeled, de-seeded and sliced

1 medium onion, chopped

6 tomatoes, skinned, de-seeded and chopped

200g potatoes, peeled and chopped

600ml chicken stock

Olive oil

Salt and pepper

Ingredients

Spinach soup

500g fresh baby leaf spinach

1 medium onion, chopped

200g potatoes, peeled

600ml chicken stock

Method (Peppers)

1　Sauté the onion and garlic for 6–8 minutes in a little olive oil, stirring all the time. Add the peppers and tomato and stir all together.

2　Add the chicken stock, which must be hot, to the mixture. Bring to the boil, add the potato and then simmer for 15–20 minutes.

3　Season with salt and pepper, put it into a blender and blend for 2–3 minutes until nice and smooth. Keep warm

Method (Spinach)

1　Sauté the onion for 6–8 minutes in a little olive oil. Add the spinach and continue to sauté until it has wilted, stirring occasionally. Add the stock (hot) to the pan and bring to the boil, turn down to a simmer and add the potato.

2　Simmer for 15–20 minutes, then season with salt and pepper.

3　Put it into a blender and blend until smooth. Keep warm

Two into one!

Here's the exciting bit: place the two soups into separate jugs, take a deep breath and gently pour both of them into the same bowl simultaneously, from opposite sides of the dish. As both soups have the same density they should each fill exactly half of the bowl. Good luck!

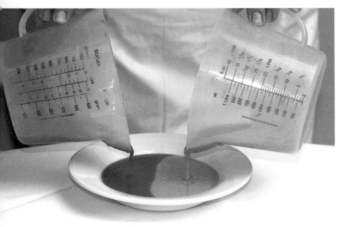

"This soup, which is really two soups in one, always turns heads and really does taste as good as it looks. The duo effect is created by making the soups slightly thicker than normal, by including potato in both recipes."

RIVELINO RODRIGUES, SOUS CHEF.

Tris of Guernsey crab

Tris di granchio

Three different flavours of chancre crab. Each recipe serves four people as a starter or two people as a main course. For a starter, aim for 100g of the completed dish per serving, or 200g for a main course.

Crab with spring onion and balsamic vinegar

400g of Guernsey chancre crab

4 spring onions, thinly sliced

25ml balsamic vinegar

50ml olive oil

½ tsp sugar

Salt and black pepper, to season

Gently mix the ingredients together, trying not to break up the crab meat too much. Serve on salad leaves tossed in your favourite dressing.

Crab with lime and coriander

400g of Guernsey chancre crab

Zest and juice of 2 limes

1 tbsp fresh coriander, chopped

Juice of 1 lemon

75ml olive oil

Salt and black pepper, to season

Gently mix together in a bowl and serve as above.

Crab with red pepper and lemongrass

400g of Guernsey chancre crab

2 red peppers, roasted, skinned and de-seeded

75ml olive oil

4 sticks of lemongrass (small and split lengthways)

Juice of 1 lemon

½ tbsp of English mustard

Bring the oil to a simmer, take off the heat and add the lemongrass. Leave overnight, to infuse.

Strain the infused oil into a food processor. Add the peppers, lemon juice, mustard and blend to a fine purée. Pass through a fine sieve and season. Gently mix together in a bowl and serve as above.

"Chancre, which is known as 'edible crab' in mainland Britain, is perhaps the number one shellfish in Guernsey. It's the authentic, traditional taste of the islands and the basis of so many delicious starters. Here are my three favourite ways of serving it. If you have a large dinner party you could prepare all three and offer each guest a taster of each. However you choose to share it this is a winner!"

TIM VIDAMOUR

Dry fried scallops gremolata

Cappesante alla gremolata

SERVES FOUR PEOPLE AS A STARTER OR TWO AS A MAIN COURSE

Ingredients

16 fresh scallops, out of their shells (four per person – or six each if small scallops)

100g of fresh ginger, peeled and roughly chopped

6 cloves of garlic, peeled and roughly chopped

2 red and 2 green chillies (medium size, seeds removed)

1 tbsp fresh coriander, chopped

Juice and finely chopped zest of 1 lemon

50ml Olive oil

Method

1 Place the ginger, garlic, chillies, coriander and lemon zest into a blender and whizz for 2–3 minutes until finely chopped (but not creamed!). Add the zest and juice of the lemon, mix and then season.

2 Place into a jar and add just enough olive oil (about 50ml) to cover the mixture. Put a lid on and place in the fridge, to let the flavours mix (this can be done the day before and will keep for 6–8 weeks in the fridge if kept covered in the olive oil).

3 Dry fry the scallops, i.e. fry using as little oil as possible, for 2–3 minutes on each side. They should be slightly undercooked but well coloured (avoid overcooking, which can make them a bit rubbery).

4 Pour 4 teaspoons of the gremolata oil onto the scallops in the pan, when they are nearly cooked. Toss quickly and serve with a few dressed leaves.

"Gremolata is an Italian term used to describe any number of ingredients, which have been finely chopped and sprinkled over a dish when it is nearly cooked"

RIVELINO RODRIGUES, SOUS CHEF

Warm canon of lamb with roasted pepper salad and anchovy cream

Agnello con peperoni e crema d'acciughe

SERVES FOUR PEOPLE AS A STARTER

Ingredients

2 canons of lamb each weighing about 200g

For the salad:

1 red pepper, 1 yellow pepper and 1 green pepper, roasted, peeled, de-seeded and sliced

A handful of mixed leaves

A handful of rocket leaves

Mix and dress in a bowl, with vinaigrette

For the anchovy cream:

1 small tin of anchovy fillets

2 cloves garlic

25g pine nuts

100ml olive oil

Lemon juice, to taste

1 tbsp chopped parsley

Method

1 Blend the anchovies, garlic and pine nuts together in a food processor, adding the olive oil in a steady stream. Add the lemon juice and stir in the parsley – it should have the consistency of double cream.

2 Meanwhile, seal the canons of lamb in a frying pan and place into a warm oven for 6–8 minutes.

3 Arrange the dressed leaves on a plate. Slice the lamb, place on top and drizzle with anchovy cream. (Each canon will serve 2 people.)

"I stumbled across this recipe some time ago. We like it so much that it keeps finding its way back onto the restaurant's monthly specials. It always goes down well, especially with hungry yachtsmen!"

TIM VIDAMOUR

A DAY IN THE LIFE ... 11.15 a.m.

"Just get him up here!" warns the head chef. The menu meeting ran on (again) and now the tasting session is late. A stray waiter bounds up the stairs and melts sheepishly into the crowd.

"...The lamb works best with the thyme and lemon pesto, so don't let customers order it without," the sous chef warns the multinational gathering. "These are pine nuts, remember," he raises a cautionary finger. "Allergies. Let the customer know".

Talking over, everyone grabs forks and hacks at the dishes, chewing, nodding and airing views in a flurry of languages and cutlery. Empty plates are quickly replaced by staff lunch, a work-a-day version of a Da Nello classic. Front and back-of-house chow-down together, bolting food, slurping coke and pausing only to trade jibes. Seven minutes to lift off. The restaurant mobile chirrups: tonight's party of 20 has finally rung back. Oh, and now they're 12.

"Thank you for letting us know", replies the restaurant manager between mouthfuls, recalling the half-hour spent shifting tables at midnight. The saletta will need completely reorganising. That'll make someone happy.

But that can wait. The headwaiter is staring at the ceiling over table one.

Drip, drip......

The restaurant manager trots upstairs to find the problem. Of course fifteenth century buildings spring leaks, but why is it always just before lunch? The Frenchman positions an ice bucket while the Slovak hastily mops the wet marble with a floor-cloth under his shoe in a ludicrous, one-man tango. Two minutes and counting.

The head hostess is ready behind the bar, but the music isn't. She watches the headwaiter sceptically as he jabs at the computerised machine. Finally, the sigh of a saxophone floats across the bar, followed swiftly by the proprietor's voice.

"We're an Italian restaurant. Let's find something Italian please. Jazz is for later."

The headwaiter rubs his chin and stares anxiously at the console.

The restaurant manger has returned: "It's the flat upstairs. I've turned the water off but we need a plumber this afternoon. At the latest." Things are looking up. One minute to go. The pavement-scrubbing waitress brings bad news: the music wasn't playing just now in the courtyard.

"It was last night."

"Maybe, but not today."

Ten seconds, ignition on. A sonorous, Neapolitan voice booms across the bar.

"That's better," nods the proprietor.

Someone has inadvertently stumbled across the right music.

The headwaiter saunters to the front door, adjusts his cuffs and checks his watch – 12.00. *Open*. We have lift off.

Roasted sweet balsamic onions

Cipolle balsamico agro-dolce

SERVES FOUR PEOPLE AS A STARTER

Ingredients

16 baby onions (peeled, 4 each)

8 slices of Parma ham

8 slices of tomato

8 slices of Mozzarella di bufala

4 slices of ciabatta bread

1 clove of garlic

3 tbsp of olive oil

2 tbsp balsamic vinegar

2 tbsp Demerara sugar

Salt and pepper

4 leaves of fresh basil (to garnish)

Method

1 Heat a large, heavy bottomed frying pan, pour in the olive oil, add the onions and fry until golden brown (turning occasionally) for 5–8 minutes. Place into a roasting tin, season with salt and black pepper and add the Balsamic vinegar and sugar. Cover with tin foil and place into a hot oven (200°C) for 15–20 minutes until cooked.

2 Once cooked, take out of the oven and put to one side to keep warm while you put the rest of the ingredients onto the plates. Place two slices of Parma ham at the top of the plate, with the slices of tomato and Mozzarella arranged alternately on one side. Spoon on the onions with some of the oil and Balsamic mixture.

3 Toast the ciabatta bread, rub with a clove of garlic and drizzle with a little olive oil. Arrange on the plate and garnish with some torn basil leaves.

"A doctor once advised my father to eat plenty of cooked onions and garlic. He soon grew tired of boiled onions, so my mother used to feed him a dish very similar to this, which he found a welcome relief. I had no idea just how successful this simple starter would be when we first tried it on the à la carte menu. It's one that you can eat day after day and never tire of it. It's particularly good with a dry fruity white wine, like Rodaro Sauvignon, which can take the acidity of the onions and vinegar."

NELLO CIOTTI

Carpaccio of beef with rocket lettuce and flakes of Parmesan

Carpaccio di manzo con rucola e Parmigiano

SERVES FOUR PEOPLE

Ingredients

400g fillet beef

1 50g tin of anchovy fillets

4 small handfuls of rocket lettuce

Olive oil

24 capers or caper berries

Juice of a lemon

150g Parmesan cheese (use a fresh, whole piece. If you have any left you can grate it over your pasta)

Method

1 Make a hole lengthways through the fillet of beef with a skewer and push 2 or 3 anchovy fillets inside. Repeat about 4 times, until you have used the whole tin. Wrap the beef in cling film and place it in the freezer for 1½ hours, to make it easier to slice.

2 Place a handful of washed rocket leaves on each plate and add Italian dressing (¼ wine vinegar, ¾ virgin olive oil).

3 Take the beef from the freezer (it should be cold but not frozen) and use a sharp knife to slice it as thinly as you can, laying the slices directly onto the plates. Keep cutting until it is all sliced and arranged on the plates. Drizzle with a little olive oil and lemon juice.

4 Flake the parmesan, using a potato peeler, and place 6 caper berries on each plate. Decorate with 2–3 rocket leaves in the centre and serve immediately.

★ Tip: Cut the beef as thin as you can then cover the slices in cling film and pat gently with a flat object or rolling pin.

"According to legend, Carpaccio was invented in Harry's Bar, in Venice. Apparently a lady customer had been advised by her doctor to eat raw meat, as she lacked iron, so the restaurant manager devised this just for her. There have been many variations on the original theme since then, including fish dishes."

NELLO CIOTTI

Linguine lobster

Linguine all'astaco

SERVES FOUR PEOPLE AS A STARTER OR TWO AS A MAIN COURSE

Ingredients

400g fresh Guernsey lobster meat (2 live lobsters weighing approx 500g each)

300g of fresh linguine (Either make it or buy from Bella's Delicatessen)

250ml Thermidor sauce (see page 111)

150ml Salsa Napolitana (Napoli sauce) (see page 112)

100ml of single Guernsey cream

"This idea is also from a 'ristorante di grido', which is how Italians describe a 'Serie A', or Premier League, eatery. The original version was a bit disappointing, not to mention eye-wateringly expensive, so we decided to do something better and more affordable. We must have succeeded because if we have such a thing as a signature dish this is it."

TIM VIDAMOUR

Method

1 Start by cooking the lobsters. Bring a large pan of water to the boil. Place the live lobsters in the water, cover and simmer for 10–12 minutes. Remove from the water and leave to cool.

2 When cold, cut the lobsters in half lengthways. Discard the head, remove the flesh from the claws and tails and put to one side. Keep the tail shells to use as a garnish. Cut the lobster into 2.5cm pieces.

Seeing old ladies boiling live shellfish in big dustbins was an everyday sight in St Peter Port's old fish market. As a boy I remember the roaring burners, the delicious smell and the constant chatter of Guernsey French. But have no fear: if you can't face doing it yourself then your fishmonger will cook them for you – if you ask nicely.

3 Pour the Thermidor and Napoli sauces into a large, deep pan and reduce to half their volume, stirring constantly. Add the cream and reduce again until you are left with a smooth, silky sauce. Add the cooked lobster.

4 In the meantime, cook the pasta in salted water with a little olive oil. Strain the pasta and add to the sauce and the cooked lobster.

5 Divide equally between the four bowls, garnish each with half a lobster tail shell and serve immediately.

★ Tip: fresh pasta is cooked when it just begins to float to the top. But be warned; it cooks much quicker than dried pasta.

Crab thermidor

Granchio thermidor

SERVES SIX PEOPLE

Ingredients

600g of freshly picked Guernsey chancre crab

250ml of Thermidor sauce (see page 111)

125ml single Guernsey cream

200g of grated Gruyere cheese

Six sprigs of continental parsley

Method

1 Prepare the Thermidor sauce, add the Guernsey cream and bring to a simmer, add 100g of the grated Gruyere cheese and keep stirring. Reduce the mixture like this until you have a rich, light yellow, silky sauce.

2 Mix in the crab and then divide it between six deep dishes.

3 Sprinkle with the remainder of the grated cheese and place under a hot grill until brown (or 'gratinated').

4 Garnish with sprigs of continental parsley.

"This is a really simple and delicious starter. To serve it as a main course, simply increase all the ingredients by half and pipe some creamed potatoes along the side of the dish, so that it browns at the same time as the crab and cheese."

TIM VIDAMOUR

Vermicelli with oysters in Champagne sauce

Vermicelli con ostriche e Champagne

SERVES FOUR PEOPLE AS A STARTER OR TWO PEOPLE AS A MAIN COURSE

Ingredients

12 oysters (Guernsey – or even Jersey! – oysters are wonderful but any large, fresh ones will do)

200g fresh vermicelli

2 glasses Champagne (save the rest of the bottle to drink with your starter)

1 glass dry white wine

100ml Guernsey cream

$\frac{1}{2}$ tbsp olive oil

1ltr salted water per 100g of pasta

4 tsps Lumpfish roe to garnish

Method

1   Open, or 'shuck' the oysters over a fine sieve (place the sieve on top of a soup plate to catch any broken shells whilst saving the juices) and pour the juice into a pan. There's definitely a knack to shucking oysters. Ask your fishmonger to show you how to do it. Place the oysters on a plate and wash the shells.

2   Pour the champagne and wine into a pan, add the oyster water and bring to the boil. Reduce by half and then add the cream. Reduce again until it becomes a light cream sauce.

3   Meanwhile, cook the pasta carefully (see page 117). Drain when ready and place a forkful of vermicelli into each oyster shell, arranging three on each plate.

4   Place the oysters into the cream sauce (with any remaining juice) and bring to the boil. Remove the oysters as soon as the sauce boils (don't overcook them) and place one oyster on top of each serving of pasta.

5   Reduce the sauce until light and creamy, adding more Champagne if it's too thick. Season and pour onto the oysters. Garnish with lumpfish roe and small sprigs of fresh dill.

"This dish can also be made with very thin pasta, such as angel hair, or with fresh linguine. If you get it right it's superb!"

TIM VIDAMOUR

A DAY IN THE LIFE ... 12.45 p.m.

Lunch is mad: so many people who all need feeding in the same hour. A busy lunch can quickly turn a gently simmering kitchen into a shuddering pressure cooker. And it's started.

"Sit down table seven!" The head chef's voice is lost in the banging saloon doors that mark the edge of his empire. A Madeiran waitress walks the message to the bar, which is flooded in early spring sunshine. It's also awash with wool: worsted and well-cut, blue and charcoal, plain and pinstriped. Well-groomed finance industry types are grouped around the glass tables, talking, waving hands and forgetting their menus. The restaurant manager hovers, hoping to catch an eye.

He takes the message and turns instead to a dapper, lone figure in the corner, signalling with a slight tilt of the head. The gentleman responds by draining his dry Martini, biting the olive from the stick and squeezing out of the corner, gathering up a jumble of magazines. Wine is waiting, on ice, at his usual table. No words are necessary. That comes later. Relaxed and easy, anecdotes, jokes, local politics.

Another four have arrived bearing overcoats, which are whisked upstairs. Coats are a curse. It's the time of year when they transform the cramped cloakroom into an ill-lit pantomime costume cupboard. They all look the same. Roll on summer.

The proprietor is working the bar, shooting greetings and lobbing jokes like indirect free kicks into the huddled tables. He commiserates over last night's surprise score-line, then finds a gap in the defence, they're ready to order. You can spot the hosts in each party. They already know what they want, lobster linguine, grilled brill, calamari with chilli and garlic. It's what they eat when they bring the family. Oh, and a few of those zucchini.

They recommend fish dishes to their guests, whose heads swivel between menu, proprietor and 'specials' blackboard. So much fish...

And to drink? Some deals work better with wine. For others, just add water. These guys are on a schedule so it's strictly San Pellegrino.

"Pity", adds the crestfallen chalk stripe, handing back the wine list. Out of the semis on penalties... He'd love to drown his sorrows.

Some visitors have arrived on a tip off from the taxi driver. Can we do a two? Certainly. They follow the headwaiter straight to a quiet corner table.

A crowd of businessmen are pointing and grinning like schoolboys at the rooftop lingerie line as they sit down at table 21. The restaurant manager pulls the cork from their bottle of Amarone.

Schloppp!

This is the other kind of deal.

MAIN COURSES
Piatti Grandi

Local line-caught bass Livornese

Branzino alla Livornese

SERVES FOUR PEOPLE AS A MAIN COURSE

Ingredients

4 225g bass fillets, skinned

200ml Salsa Napolitana (see page 112)

24 caper berries (alternatively, you could use pitted, halved black olives)

1 tsp finely chopped garlic

Juice of 1 lemon

1 tbsp of chopped Italian parsley

½ glass of dry white wine

Salt and pepper

Method

1   Dry fry the bass, i.e. fry using as little oil as possible, for three minutes on each side. Place the fillets either in individual dishes or on a large roasting tray. Season with salt and pepper.

2   Pour the white wine, Napoli sauce and lemon juice on top of the bass. Add the garlic, parsley and caper berries. Cover with tin foil and place in a hot oven (200°C) for 15 minutes, until cooked.

3   Don't remove the tin foil until you present the bass on the table, so that your guests can savour that magnificent aroma!

"There are several small variations on this recipe, but this is one that has built up a loyal following amongst our regular customers."

NELLO CIOTTI

Brill with saffron and mussel sauce

Rombetto con zafferano e cozze

SERVES FOUR PEOPLE

Ingredients

4 225g fresh Guernsey brill fillets, skinned

150ml fish stock (see page 111)

100ml white wine

50ml Noilly Prat or any dry, white vermouth

50ml white wine vinegar

1 shallot, finely chopped

150ml single Guernsey cream

5g saffron powder

50g Guernsey butter, cut into small cubes

450g mussels, washed and cleaned

Salt

A pinch of cayenne pepper

Method

1 Place the stock, white wine, shallot and vinegar into a pan and bring to the boil. Reduce by a half. Add the saffron and mussels. Simmer until the mussels have just opened. Strain, keeping the sauce and the mussels separately. Let the liquid stand so that any grit settles at the bottom

2 Pour the sauce back into the pan, taking care not to include any grit. Add the cream and cayenne pepper. Reduce the sauce until light and creamy and keep warm. Finally, add the mussels, which you have taken out of their shells (leave 24 of them in their shells, to use as a garnish – 6 per plate).

3 In the meantime, dry fry the brill, i.e. fry using as little oil as possible, for 3–4 minutes on each side, then place into a medium oven (160°C) for 8–10 minutes until cooked. Whisk the butter into the sauce, season and add the mussels in their shells.

4 Serve on plain, steamed spinach, with mashed potatoes.

"We borrowed this recipe from a famous restaurant in north Brittany and enjoyed it so much that we decided not to give it back!"
NELLO CIOTTI

Guernsey lobster with orange

Astago all'arancia

SERVES TWO PEOPLE

Ingredients

2 live lobsters, each weighing a little over 500g. (N.B. Use a live lobster to get the best from this recipe. However, you can use a cooked lobster if you prefer – just don't cook it for the first 6–8 minutes of the recipe. Carry on with making the sauce in the same way.)

1 tbsp virgin olive oil

50ml Cognac

100ml fresh orange juice

30g Guernsey butter

50ml of fish stock (see page 111)

1 tbsp chopped Italian parsley

Salt and pepper

Method

1   Place the oil into a large, heated frying pan. Cut the lobster (live or cooked) in half down the middle and crack the claws with a hammer.

2   Carefully add the lobster to the pan, flesh downwards, cover with a lid and cook for 6–8 minutes on a medium heat. Remove the lid and flambé with Cognac. Add the orange juice and fish stock and reduce for 3–4 minutes. Remove lobster and cool.

3   Add the butter and reduce to make the sauce richer. Meanwhile take lobster out of shell and chop. Add the lobster to the sauce and, when hot, spoon back into the shell, sprinkle with chopped parsley and serve.

"You could create this dish using other lobsters, but, for me, it's got to be Guernsey. You can't beat the real thing."

TIM VIDAMOUR

Monkfish wrapped in Parma ham with truffle oil

Involtini di coda di rospo al prosciutto di Parma e olio al tartufo

SERVES FOUR PEOPLE AS A MAIN COURSE

Ingredients

4 225g monkfish tails (ask your fishmonger – nicely! – to clean them for you)

2 sprigs of dill

4 good slices of Parma ham (8 slices if they are small)

Olive oil

White truffle oil (I get mine from Oil & Vinegar)

For the vegetables:

8 spring onions, finely chopped

500g fresh, baby spinach

200g peas

1 glass of white wine

75g Guernsey butter

Salt and pepper

Method

1. Place ½ a sprig of dill on each monkfish tail. Roll each tail in a slice of Parma ham and place in the fridge on a plate for 20 minutes, to bond the ham to the fish (it also helps to use cocktail sticks but remember to remove them before serving).

2. When they are ready, pan fry the monkfish tails in a little olive oil for 4–5 minutes on each side and then place into a hot oven (180°C) for 10–12 minutes, until cooked.

3. Meanwhile, sauté the spring onion in a pan with a little olive oil for 4–5 minutes, until soft, then add the peas and white wine.

4. Add the butter, season and reduce until nearly all the wine has evaporated. Now add the spinach; as soon as it wilts the dish is ready. Arrange the vegetables and monkfish on the plate as shown in the photograph and drizzle with truffle oil.

"This recipe found its way to number 46 Le Pollet via a famous television chef, who worked in Italy for a while and dined in Da Nello a few times."
NELLO CIOTTI

Dry fried scallops with balsamic syrup and crispy pancetta

Capesante allo sciroppo balsamico e pancetta

SERVES FOUR PEOPLE

Ingredients

28 fresh scallops, out of their shells

8 slices of pancetta

¼ cup Balsamic vinegar

1 cup red wine

1 tbsp sugar

500g fresh baby spinach leaves

Salt

Black pepper

Method

1 Make the syrup by mixing the balsamic vinegar, red wine and sugar together in a pan. Bring to the boil and simmer until the mixture coats the back of a wooden spoon. Put to one side and leave to cool. If the syrup is too thick, add a little water and reheat. You should be able to pour it into a squeezy bottle and keep it out of the fridge until needed.

2 Place the pancetta on a grilling tray under a hot grill, until crispy. Meanwhile, dry fry the scallops. To do this heat a non-stick pan and drizzle in some olive oil. As soon as the oil is hot, pour the excess away leaving just enough to lubricate the pan. Place the scallops in the pan and dry fry like this for 2–3 minutes on each side.
For the best flavour, leave the scallops slightly undercooked.

3 Share the spinach leaves between the four plates, lay the scallops on top (the heat will wilt the leaves) and season with salt and black pepper. Place the crispy pancetta on top and then drizzle the balsamic syrup over the scallops. Serve immediately.

★ Tip: Balsamic syrup is perfect on most grilled meats and plain fish and will keep for weeks – provided it is not stored in the fridge. It is also delicious on strawberries, with a dusting of black pepper.

A DAY IN THE LIFE ... 2.30 p.m.

"We had some coats and a small leather case. Oh, and a laptop". The head hostess smiles sweetly and slips away to the quick-change cupboard. Two of these men have flights to catch. One, a tall Swiss-German, is discussing skiing with the proprietor, in Italian, when she returns under a heap of dark cloth.

"Thank you, arrivederci, buon viaggio".

They step straight into the waiting taxi, which has been blocking a convoy of delivery vans, and disappear. A van stops at the door and a small, bearded figure jumps out, slides open the side door, swings a bulbous white sack onto his back and scurries up to the waiters' station. Clean linen for tonight's big push.

"Cheerie" he shouts to no one in particular as he dashes back out to an even worse traffic jam.

The head hostess is muttering, scribbling bills and slipping them into padded folders for the waiters to deliver.

"How many bottles of wine on table 12?"

No one answers. She rolls her eyes and goes to check, passing the sous chef and chef de partie as they leave in search of a few hours peace.

The headwaiter is reloading a wine fridge, squeezing extra bottles into a corner. It's Friday, so cold Pinot Grigio will be like gold dust tonight. The phone rings.

"Hello, Da Nello? Four for tonight? Hmm… I haven't got anything until later. Nine o'clock? Certainly, what's the name?"

Bills, ledgers and Guernsey banknotes cover the bar table as the restaurant manager rechecks last night's till readings. This job is best done first thing in the morning but today's menu meeting scuppered that. It's his second attempt when the head hostess calls him. The tall, blonde girl at the bar would like to buy a meal voucher for her sister's birthday. Certainly. He arranges the piles of paper and goes to retrieve the voucher book.

"Thanks. Bye. Thank you very much". Waiters beam and open doors for a stream of bankers, lawyers, visitors and retired regulars, who button their coats and head back to their business or pleasure. The girl leaves clutching her voucher and the restaurant manager resumes his hunt for the missing twelve pounds.

Found it! He bundles papers into envelopes. Just the music left to sort out in the top rooms. The Slovakian waiter appears with raised eyebrows and an empty bottle.

"Another Amarone on 21!" he announces, scribbling a chit for the head hostess.

The restaurant manager sighs. Table 21 is smack in the middle of the music-free zone. Any repair will have to wait until they've gone.

"Wotcha! Where's your leak?" It's the cavalry, clad in a red boiler suit and clutching a plumber's bag.

Grigliata of the best of Guernsey fish

Grigliata di pesce locale

SERVES TWO PEOPLE

Ingredients

Fish

1 live lobster (560g approx)

1 fillet of brill, cut in half (225–250g)

1 fillet of bass, cut in half (225–250g)

4 scallops

2 king prawns, with their shells on

Ingredients

Marinade mix

100ml olive oil

Juice of half a lemon

2 cloves of crushed garlic

1 chopped carrot

6 whole black peppercorns

1 tsp of chopped dill, sorrel and parsley

Method

1 30 minutes before cooking, place the brill, bass, scallops and king prawns in a large bowl. Pour on the marinade mix, toss the fish to ensure it's well coated, cover and place in the fridge.

2 Cut the lobster in half lengthways and crack the claws with a hammer. Warm the oven to 200°C. Lay the lobster in a roasting tray, flesh side up, drizzle with a little olive oil and place in the oven for 10–12 minutes.

3 Heat a griddle pan to red hot – bluish smoke will appear. Remove the fish from the marinade and pour the liquid away. Place the brill and bass into the griddle pan and sear for 2–3 minutes on each side, plus the scallops and prawns for 2 minutes on each side.

4 Finish cooking the fish by putting the griddle in the oven with the lobster for the final 5–6 minutes. Divide onto 2 hot plates, drizzle the juice from the tray on top, serve with lemon wedges, new potatoes and mixed salad.

"This dish is what Da Nello is all about: wonderful, fresh Guernsey fish, cooked on the charcoal grill, each with its own individual flavour. Forget any sauce: it just confuses the taste. Just add a squeeze of lemon and, if you fancy, a trickle of good olive oil. It's so simple. I love it."

NELLO CIOTTI

Braised lamb shank in Marsala wine

Brasato di stinco d'Agnello al Marsala

SERVES FOUR PEOPLE

Ingredients

4 lamb shanks, just as they come from your butcher

4 cloves of garlic, finely chopped

2 shallots, finely chopped

3 medium sized carrots, finely chopped

2 stalks of celery, finely chopped

100ml of Marsala wine

400g of tinned tomatoes, with their juice

1 tbsp chopped parsley

Juice and zest of an orange and a lemon

Method

1 Fry all the vegetable together in a pan, for 8-10 minutes, and then place them in a deep roasting tray. Season with salt and black pepper.

2 Add the juice and zest (finely chopped) of the orange and the lemon.

3 Pass the lamb shanks through seasoned flour and pan fry in a little olive oil. Keep turning them until sealed and have a nice golden brown colour. Place the shanks on top of the vegetables and season again with salt and black pepper.

4 Take the pan that you have cooked the lamb in, put it on a medium heat and pour in the Marsala, tomatoes and juice. Stir around the whole pan with a wooden spoon (a technique known as 'deglazing'). Add a pinch of sugar and chopped parsley and then pour over the lamb shanks. Cover with tin foil and place in a moderate oven (180°C) for 1¾ hours.

5 This is a dish that can be prepared a couple of days before you serve it, so, when it's cold, skim off any fat that floats to the top. Then cover and reheat in a moderate oven (180°C) for 40 minutes. Serve with olive oil mashed potato.

"This is always well received in the restaurant. The recipe was suggested by my wife Della, who reads about food more than she cooks it and has a real eye for wholesome, well presented dishes."

NELLO CIOTTI

Veal cutlet with thyme and lemon pesto

Cotoletta di vitello al pesto

SERVES FOUR PEOPLE

Ingredients

4 veal cutlets, each weighing approx 300g (you may have to pre-order from your butcher, who can also cut them to size for you)

Pesto sauce (see page 116)

A handful of thyme finely chopped

2 cloves of garlic finely chopped

Juice and finely chopped zest of a lemon

Salt and pepper

Method

1   Pour the pesto into a bowl. Add the thyme and garlic as well as the zest and juice of the lemon. Season if needed. Pour into a jar and cover with a little olive oil. Put the lid on and place it in the fridge (this can be done several days before and will keep for 6–8 weeks in the fridge).

2   Char-grill the veal cutlets – we have a char grill but you can use a barbecue or a grill pan. Cook on each side for 4-5 minutes on a medium heat, taking care not to burn the meat, then place on a roasting tray. Pour a dessert spoon of pesto onto each cutlet and place in a medium heat oven (180°C) for 4–5 minutes to leave the veal pinkish.

3   Serve with olive oil mashed potatoes and char-grilled aubergines

"Veal cutlets are a firm favourite on the Italian dinner table and always excellent. My advice is to find a good butcher and stick with him."
NELLO CIOTTI

Escalope of veal with Vin Santo wine and Muscat grapes

Scalloppine di vitello al Vin Santo con uva Moscata

SERVES FOUR PEOPLE

Ingredients

4 150g veal escalopes

50ml olive oil

150ml Vin Santo dessert wine

200g jar or tin of Muscat grapes, or any fresh, small grapes, halved and de-seeded

2 tbsp flour, sieved and seasoned

1 glass white wine

100g Guernsey butter

1 tsp chopped parsley

Method

1 Start by beating the escalope of veal. To do this, put the meat between 2 pieces of cling film and hit it gently with a meat hammer or rolling pin until it is thin. Be careful not to strike it too hard or the meat will shred and break. Place the pieces of meat on a plate and put it in the fridge.

2 Drizzle some olive oil in a large pan and heat on a medium flame until hot. Pass the veal through seasoned flour and pan fry for 2–3 minutes on each side. Place the escalope of veal in an ovenproof dish and keep warm. Drain off the excess oil from the pan and then add the white wine, Vin Santo and the butter.

3 Turn the flame up high to reduce the sauce in the pan to a smooth consistency. Add the grapes, season with salt and black pepper. Arrange the veal on warm plates and spoon over the sauce. Sprinkle with parsley and serve with your favourite potatoes and vegetables.

"This is a very quick dish, so you need to be well prepared. The aim is, literally, to cook and eat it."

TIM VIDAMOUR

Medallions of beef Barolo

Medaglioni di manzo al Barolo

SERVES FOUR PEOPLE

Ingredients

4 fillets of beef, each weighing 225g
and cut in half crossways, to form
medallions. Buy the best beef you can
find; it will be worth it.

Method

1 The starting point for this dish is very simple: top
quality beef. However, the secret of its timeless
appeal is in the rich Barolo sauce, which features a
garlic butter base, Guernsey cream and demi glace
as well as a large glass of Barolo Piedmont's finest
red wine.

2 Char-grill or pan fry the medallions of beef to
taste (I tend not to cook them more than
'medium', to make the most of good meat), place
onto plates and cover carefully with the Barolo
sauce.

3 Serve with sauté potatoes, carrots and steamed
spinach. Enjoy!

Barolo sauce

Ingredients

2 tbsp Garlic Butter (see page 113)

100ml Demi glace (see page 114)

150ml cream

1 glass of Barolo

Method

To make the Barolo sauce, heat a large frying pan,
place in the garlic butter mixture and allow it to melt.
Next, add the glass of red wine and reduce by half.
Then add the demi glace and cream and reduce until
it can coat the back of a wooden spoon.

"More than any other, beef Barolo is a dish that deserves a page in this book. It
is the only one that has featured on every Da Nello à la carte menu, right from
the start, and is still very popular. In fact I've known it for longer than I've
known my wife."

TIM VIDAMOUR

Rack of venison with red onion and Chianti sauce

Costata di cervo con salsa di cipolle rosse al Chianti

SERVES FOUR PEOPLE

Ingredients

1 rack of Scottish venison, weighing 1kg, cut into 4 racks. The rack should come very well cleaned and prepared ready for you to cut through, but you may still need to remove a minimal amount of fat or sinew.

Red onion and Chianti sauce
(see page 115)

Method

1   Heat a frying pan with a little olive oil. Place the racks of venison in the pan and fry for 2–3 minutes on each side. Put the racks on an oven proof dish and place in a medium oven (175°C) for 6–8 minutes (this will produce meat that is rare).

2   Remove from the oven when ready and leave to rest (2–3 minutes).

3   We serve it with red onion and Chianti sauce, buttered broccoli, dauphinois potatoes and a grillled tomato.

"Venison is a seasonal treat, so check whether your butcher can supply it before planning this dish. We always aim to source ours from Scotland. Not only is it top quality, but it also sounds so romantic."

TIM VIDAMOUR

A DAY IN THE LIFE ... 3.15p.m.

Mid afternoon: the dead zone, when restaurateurs are at home taking it easy, feet up in preparation for a busy night. That's the theory, which is seldom in step with reality, and today is pretty real. The restaurant manager is pacing a draughty packing shed in search of roses for tonight's onslaught. The silence is shattered by the rattle of a sliding door.

'Bon dia!' The voice comes from a bulging black bin sack, balanced on a pair of wellington boots. The smiling face peeking around the bag gives the game away. Yes, the small Portuguese lady has his order, bagged and ready. They chat and laugh, loading bundles of red, pink, yellow and orange flowers into the restaurant van. Job done. Only the store left.

Horrible! The only thing the head hostess hates more than the cold is heights. So why, she asks herself, is she clinging to a stepladder on the roof of the restaurant, wrestling with windswept lingerie in the middle of March? Da Nello's washing line is not so much a drying facility, more a local institution. The skimpiest of undergarments make enticing appearances, flanked by voluminous brassieres and occasionally supported by big name international football shirts. The long-running lascivious laundry has a tendency to amaze, amuse and distract – probably in that order. She braces herself against another gust and pegs out an unfeasibly brief pair of briefs. Where did the girls find these? ....No! A wine-red, zeppelin-sized bra breaks loose and vanishes over the glass roof. Start again...

The headwaiter watches intently from behind the bar, polishing wineglasses. The proprietor is at it again, tape measure in hand.

'Three metres thirty-six. Write that down.' The earnest sales rep scribbles the figures on his pad.

'I want to change all this seating. These chairs were great when we got them but they've been done. Everyone's got them now. Here, look...'

The proprietor grabs an order pad and biro and starts sketching. The three figures crowd around the bar counter, heads tilting this way and that as the plan unfolds.

'Oh, I see what you mean,' offers the sales rep finally. The headwaiter looks at him in amazement.

That was close! The passing truck narrowly missed the restaurant manager, who adjusts his grip on the case of Chianti. The store opens directly onto a busy St Peter Port road, which turns every pick-up and delivery into a game of chicken. He loads the bottles into the van and reaches into his pocket for the crumpled list.

Six cases of olives? Curse the kitchen!

He waits for the bellowing, souped-up hatchback to pass before darting back across the road.

Tagliata of Guernsey beef

Tagliata di manzo di Guernsey

SERVES TWO PEOPLE

Ingredients

450g Guernsey strip loin of beef (Forest Stores is good for this)

2 medium tomatoes

150g small button mushrooms

200g potatoes, cut for chips

1 tbsp chopped parsley

Serve with Béarnaise sauce (see page 115)

Method

1   Start by preparing the meat. Make 2 or 3 cuts through the fat and sinew then place it on a board and beat gently 3 or 4 times on each side with a meat hammer.

2   Grill the meat the way you like it, either on a barbecue or in a grill pan. I prefer mine medium rare, so I cook it for 6–8 minutes on each side. Remember that this is a big slab of beef, so it will take some time if you want it well cooked (you might prefer to finish it in the oven).

3   Meanwhile, season the tomatoes with salt and black pepper, drizzle with olive oil and place under a hot grill for 4–5 minutes.

4   Sauté the mushrooms in a frying pan, with olive oil, salt and black pepper. Add a teaspoon of chopped parsley when they are ready.

5   Deep fry the chips until crisp and season with salt.

6   Place the meat in the centre of a chopping board. Arrange the tomatoes, mushrooms and chips around it, as a garnish. Serve the béarnaise sauce in individual pots.

7   Slice the meat at an angle – not too thinly – with a carving knife and share between the two plates, with the vegetables. You may prefer to serve the chips in small bowls.

"'Tagliata' simply means 'cut up', as in 'Dammi una tagliata ai capelli' ('give me a haircut'). We carve this dish at the table in Da Nello, which customers seem to enjoy. It's actually a very simple dish and perfect for a home barbecue."

NELLO CIOTTI

Stuffed corn-fed chicken breast with lemon and pistachio nuts

Petto di pollo farcito con limone e pistachio

SERVES SIX PEOPLE

Ingredients

6 chicken breasts

1 glass white wine

250ml balsamic vinegar

100g Guernsey butter

300g fresh fettucine

Olive oil for frying

For the filling:

25g butter

1 onion, finely chopped

2 tsps garlic, finely chopped

2 sprigs thyme, chopped

110g pistachio nuts, shelled and blended

Zest and juice of 2 lemons

60g white breadcrumbs

10ml olive oil

A pinch of sugar

1 tbsp of chopped continental parsley

Method

1 Gently cook the onion, garlic and thyme in a pan, with a little butter and salt. Take it off the heat after five minutes and place the contents in a bowl.

2 Add the nuts, zest, lemon juice, breadcrumbs, sugar, olive oil, salt, pepper and a handful of parsley to the mixture. Stir the mixture together to create a stiff, coarse paste. Add more oil if it's too dry; if too wet, add more breadcrumbs.

3 Slit the chicken breast along the flesh, from the thicker end. Season, fill with the mixture and then close the breast. Pass the chicken through seasoned flour and fry in a little olive oil, finishing it off in the oven (15–20 minutes).

4 When cooked, remove the chicken and keep warm. Strain off a little of the fat from the pan, add the white wine, balsamic vinegar and butter then reduce. Serve the chicken on the fettucine, which was cooked in boiling salted water for 6–8 minutes, and pour the sauce over it.

"Italians do not normally serve pasta and cuts of meat on the same plate, but I think this dish works well."

NELLO CIOTTI

Calves liver with whisky and pepper sauce

Fegato di vitello con salsa all'whisky e pepe

SERVES FOUR PEOPLE

Ingredients

600g sliced, fresh calves liver (4x 150g)

50ml white wine

100ml whisky

100ml demi glace (see page 114)

50ml single Guernsey cream

2 tbsp green peppercorns

3 tbsp flour, sieved and seasoned

Salt and black pepper

Method

1 Heat some olive oil in a large frying pan. Pass the pieces of liver through the seasoned flour and place them carefully in the pan. Cook for 3 minutes (or less if you prefer your liver pink) and then turn over. Add the green peppercorns and seasoning.

2 Cook for 1 minute, remove from the pan and keep warm. Add the white wine to the pan, reduce. Pour in the whisky and then flambé (technical way of saying 'set fire to it').

3 Let the flames die down and then add the demi glace and cream.

4 Reduce the sauce to a smooth consistency and season to taste.

5 Arrange the liver on warmed plates and spoon the pepper sauce on top.

6 Serve with sauté potatoes (my favourite), carrots and broccoli.

"Don't attempt this dish with anything other than calves liver. It has to be the real thing."

TIM VIDAMOUR

Risotto Milanese

SERVES SIX PEOPLE AS A MAIN COURSE

Ingredients

70g butter

1 onion, chopped

500g rice

1 glass dry white wine

1ltr consommé (good quality chicken or vegetable stock cubes can be used)

1 good pinch saffron strands

100g grated Parmesan cheese

Method

1 Sauté the finely chopped onion in 40g of the butter until translucent. Add rice, wine and some of the consommé and let the rice absorb it while stirring continuously.

2 Now add the saffron (which you have previously soaked in a little warm water) and the remaining consommé. As soon as the rice is just cooked (just under 20 minutes), or as Italians call it *al dente*, take it off the stove and add the remaining 30g of butter and the Parmesan.

3 Cover and let it stand for 3–4 minutes (this method is known as *mantecare*), then stir well to mix all the flavours. Serve immediately.

"This is a legendary rice dish and it's vital that you use Italian arborio rice and top quality saffron. The classic Milanese also has a finely chopped piece of beef marrow, which makes the risotto a little creamier. Ask your butcher for about 50g of marrow for this quantity and add it to the pan, with the onion. To create a tasty vegetarian version, simply leave out the bone marrow and use a vegetable stock."

TIM VIDAMOUR

A DAY IN THE LIFE ... 6.20 p.m.

The metallic melody chimes for the third time in as many minutes.

'Hello Da Nello'.

The proprietor has just finished dinner at home, but the restaurant phone is still diverted to his mobile.

'Two for tomorrow night?' The caller is in luck, bagging the last free table.

'See you at six thirty tomorrow.'

He scribbles the details in his diary and climbs into the car for the short drive to St Peter Port.

The sous chef is clearing the staff dinner plates with the chef de partie as the rest of the kitchen staff go to action stations. 120 booked, including two big parties; it's going to be fast and furious. Two waitresses are at the service station, folding napkins. The Slovak waiter should be helping but instead is showing off his new mobile phone to the Frenchman.

'Full Internet, no?' the Slovak beams, pumping buttons.

He is rewarded with a shrug of Gallic insouciance.

The headwaiter is busy placing rattling steel buckets in corners and on granite ledges. There can never be enough ice buckets on nights like this.

The proprietor is in the bar with the final booking lists. The restaurant manager copies them onto the table plan, which is a jumble of corrections, names, Tipp-ex and numbers. They study it together and make the final pencil and rubber adjustments. Finished, but that's just the start. The plan will bend and stretch as the night unfurls, morphing to accommodate late arrivals, extended groups and lucky 'chances': the name given to prospective diners who arrive unannounced. Not much hope tonight, unless there's a 'no show'. The restaurant manager makes three copies of the plan with the fax machine and passes them to the head hostess, who hurriedly glues them to pieces of card. The waiters gather round; this is the musical score that will set the tempo for tonight's performance, even if Fridays are more like modern jazz.

The first two tables arrive bang on 6.30. That's a good sign. A few delays now can send the whole evening spiralling out of control. Table 12 is a local family with two young boys, still in school uniform. Table three is a regular, a lone businessman who devours thick and intriguing history books while he eats. He's amiable and well travelled but no one is sure whether he's English or Russian. A waitress squats down and rearranges one of the bar fridges, making room for a couple of extra bottles of Pinot Grigio. She knows there are never enough on nights like this.

The first party is here, with lots of wet coats. They are nearly all regulars, celebrating a 50th birthday. Lots of kissing and shaking hands with the proprietor and restaurant manager.

'It's horrible out there!' a lady exclaims, as she hands over a dripping brolly.

A blonde girl in a long overcoat squeezes behind the party, unnoticed.

'Buona sera,' she offers to no one in particular and heads straight for the stairs. Reinforcements for the bar.

DESSERTS

Dolci

Mascarpone and ginger cheesecake

Torta di zenzero e mascarpone

SERVES TEN PEOPLE

Ingredients

For the biscuit base:

240g ginger snap biscuits, crushed in a blender

120g unsalted Guernsey butter, melted

For the filling:

500g Philadelphia cream cheese

250g mascarpone cheese

180g caster sugar

2 eggs, beaten

4 whole pieces of stem ginger in syrup, finely chopped. These are sold in bottles, with each piece roughly the size and shape of a pickled onion

50g fresh ginger, grated

Method

1 Heat the oven to 180°C. Melt the butter, mix together with the biscuits and press into a 24cm spring-form cake tin. Bake the biscuit base for 10 minutes in the oven then take out and leave to cool. Turn down the oven to 160°C.

2 Make the filling by placing the cream cheese, mascarpone cheese, sugar, eggs, fresh and stem ginger in a blender, blending until smooth. Pour into the cake tin on top of the biscuit base and bake until the centre is set – around 45–55 minutes. Take out of the oven and place on a wire rack, to cool.

3 Divide into 10 portions, sprinkle each with caster sugar and caramelise with a blowtorch or under a hot grill.

4 Serve when cold, with fresh blueberries and mango sorbet, or slices of caramelised oranges.

"One of our customers memorably described this dessert as 'love-on-a-plate'."
NELLO CIOTTI

Prosecco and summer berry jelly

Gelatina al prosecco con frutti di bosco

SERVES SIX PEOPLE

Ingredients

12 strawberries

6 blackberries

24 blueberries

18 raspberries

1/4 pt elderflower cordial

1/2 bottle prosecco

2 tbsp sugar

4 leaves gelatine

Method

1   Place 2 strawberries, 1 blackberry, 4 blueberries and 3 raspberries into each Dariole mould (a teacup works just as well). Place in the fridge to cool.

2   Place the gelatine into a bowl for 4–5 minutes with a little cold water, to soften. Pour the elderflower cordial and sugar into a pan and bring to a simmer.

3   Drain off the water from the softened gelatine and add the gelatine to the warm cordial and sugar mix. Whisk together until the gelatine is well melted.

4   Open the prosecco, add ½ to the mixture and enjoy the rest yourself. Mix the prosecco and cordial mixture and pour onto the berries, making sure to push the berries down into the liquid. Place in the fridge and leave to set.

5   Remove the jellies from their moulds by dipping them in a bowl of hot water for 2–3 seconds and then turning them upside down. They should fall out. Decorate each one with a fresh sprig of mint and serve with Guernsey strawberry ice cream or fresh berries.

"Prosecco is the Venetians' elegant alternative to Champagne, with less of the sometimes-biting bubbles. It works well in this jelly, which is a summer favourite."

NELLO CIOTTI

Tiramisu

SERVES TEN TO TWELVE PEOPLE

Ingredients

5 eggs

250g mascarpone cheese

150ml Marsala wine

50ml white wine

2 tsp caster sugar

200g sponge fingers

2 tbsp cocoa, for dusting

100ml strong, cold coffee

Method

1   It's best to make tiramisu the day before you want to eat it, as it needs several hours in the fridge.

2   First separate the eggs, yolks in a stainless steel bowl and the whites in a mixing bowl. Whisk the whites and put both bowls in the fridge for 10-15 minutes.

3   Half fill a pan of water and bring it to a simmer. Take the bowl of egg yolks and add the sugar, white wine and 50ml of the Marsala.

4   Place the bowl on top of the pan of simmering water (bain marie) and whisk for 5–6 minutes, until the mixture froths up and becomes quite thick. Put to one side and allow to cool.

5   Meanwhile, put the mascarpone cheese and 50ml of the Marsala together in a third bowl and cream together.

6   Whisk the egg whites until soft peaks form when you lift out the whisk.
So, you now have 3 bowls:
The egg yolk mix (zabaglione)
The mascarpone and Marsala mix
The egg whites

7   Pour the zabaglione into the mascarpone and Marsala mix and cream together. Next, gently fold the egg whites into the zabaglione and mascarpone mix and place in the fridge.

8   Use a shallow dish to mix the remainder of the Marsala and the cold coffee (you can use Amaretto instead of Marsala if you prefer).

9   Make the first layer of the tiramisu by dipping sponge fingers into the coffee mix for just a couple of seconds before placing them into a spring form cake tin. Keep half of the sponge fingers for your second layer.

10 Take the zabaglione mix from the fridge and pour half of it over the first layer of sponge fingers. Repeat the whole process to build the second layer.

11 Smooth the top of the tiramisu and place it in the fridge for a minimum of 5–6 hours (overnight is best).

12 To serve, release the spring catch on the cake tin and put it onto a large plate. Dust with cocoa powder and cut at the table. Add a few candles for the perfect birthday cake.

"In Italy every housewife has her own recipe and swears by it. We are no different."
TIM VIDAMOUR

Strawberry and grenadine brûlée with mango sorbet

Crema brûlée al melagrana con fragole e con sorbetto di mango

SERVES SIX PEOPLE

Ingredients

550ml Guernsey cream

28ml grenadine

6 egg yolks

250g ripe Guernsey strawberries

125g sugar

Method

1 Half fill a pan with water and bring it to the boil. Place the cream, sugar and grenadine in a pan and heat it up without boiling. Put the egg yolks in a bowl and add the cream mix. Place the bowl on top of the pan of boiling water and whisk occasionally until the mixture coats the back of a spoon (6–8 minutes).

2 Half fill a roasting tray with water and place 6 ramekins in it. Put 2 strawberries, each cut into 4 pieces, into each ramekin.

3 When the brûlée mix is ready, pour it into the ramekins and bake in bain-marie until just set (20–30 mins approx). Take out of the bain-marie and put onto a tray to cool. Place in the fridge for 1½–2 hours. Just before serving, pour just enough sugar to cover each brûlée and caramelise them. The easiest way to do this is with a catering blowtorch, but a very hot grill will also do the trick.

4 Garnish with a cut strawberry, lightly dusted with icing sugar. Serve with mango sorbet.

Mango sorbet

Ingredients

200g sugar

125ml mango purée

1 lemon

1 egg white

375ml water

Method

1 Sorbet can be made several days before you need it. Bring the sugar, water and peeled zest of the lemon to the boil. Remove from the heat and leave to cool.

2 Add the juice of the lemon, mango purée and egg white and mix together well. Pass the mixture through a fine strainer and freeze.

★ Note: Sorbet is easy to make, but if you are looking for a ready made alternative try French Accents, at St Sampson's. Their sorbets are very good indeed.

"The ingredients change with the seasons, but there is always a brûlée on our dessert menu. They are very popular, probably because they are full of flavour and not too heavy; but not too light either! This one is my favourite and, for me, it's the taste of summer."

RIVELINO RODRIGUES, SOUS CHEF

Flour-free chocolate cake with Guernsey ice cream

Torta Caprese al cioccolato con gelato di Guernsey

SERVES TEN TO TWELVE PEOPLE

Ingredients

150g chocolate

200g unsalted Guernsey butter

200g caster sugar

200g ground almonds

5 eggs, separated

Method

1 Melt the chocolate and butter in a bowl, over a pan of boiling water (bain marie). Add the sugar and almonds and mix well.

2 Add the egg yolks and mix well.

3 Whip up the egg white and fold into the mixture. Pour the mixture into a buttered, 9 inch cake tin and bake in the oven (180°C) for 45–55 minutes. Take out of the oven and leave to cool.

4 Dust with icing sugar and serve with your favourite Guernsey ice cream.

★ Tip: Torta Caprese al cioccolato keeps well for several days out of the fridge.

"Look, no flour! This is a delicious and very versatile cake. You can either serve up a big one for afternoon tea, or a slice for dessert or cut it into 2cm squares and offer it as petit fours."

NELLO CIOTTI

A DAY IN THE LIFE … 8.30 p.m.

It's the witching hour, when the whole place shakes. Early diners linger over coffee as new arrivals clog the bar, juggling glasses and menus whilst vying for a place to sit. People make their entrances and exits like actors, with hugs, handshakes and even more of those cursed coats. Hassled waitresses pound the stairs to the overstuffed cloakroom, arms full and scarves trailing as they try to remember that last drinks order. A windswept figure in wellingtons casually saunters through to the kitchen with a sack full of fresh brill, recently hauled from the sea in his small boat. He nods, unseen, to the headwaiter, who is reassuring an elderly lady that the fish really is fresh.

The head hostess shouts over the cacophony in Italian, announcing the arrival of a four who insist they've booked. No one has heard of them. The proprietor studies the illegible table plan like a poker hand. A table has just rung in with a delay. Time for some of that improvisation. He calls to the headwaiter.

'I need table 15 for four, now!'

Stage directions are always in curt Italian. The latecomers are good customers and will probably end up with a better table. He smiles at the four.

'Certainly, your table will be ready immediately. Can we take your coats and get you something to drink?'

The headwaiter exits stage left in search of a waiter to lay the table. One glimpse of the dining room is enough to know it will be quicker to do it himself.

'Table 10 away! Sit down table eight!' The chef's bell is ringing again. The kitchen is taking a pounding but standing its ground. Two waitresses huddle together at the pass, waiting for vegetables for the 50th birthday table.

'OK, go.' The head chef whips the check from the magnetic rail and slides all the rest up. Behind him a huge tongue of flame leaps from a pan, which the sous chef is stirring quickly with a fork.

'Where is that extra spinach? I need it now.' The head chef is calm, controlled and very fast. Fridge doors slam, burners roar, oil gurgles and white cotton figures move purposefully in the steaming heat. The next 40 minutes will make or break the evening, as starter, main and sweet orders gush in as one single, unforgiving, uncontrollable torrent. 'Check on!' Here's another.

The saloon door bangs open and a diminutive waitress dumps a stack of plates onto the steel worktop. The kitchen porter falls on them like a hawk, tossing fistfuls of fish bones and twisted lemon segments into the waste bin before the waitress can start scraping the plates. He blasts the grease with a powerful armoured hose then plunges them into a trough of hot suds. If dirty plates back up then the whole system starts to break down.

Outside, the courtyard is pure theatre. Two young women are deep in conversation, oblivious to the washing line and their husbands' conspiratorial whispering. Blimey, who owns that red bra? Is she here?

The restaurant manager is carving a tagliata, the formidable two-man steak, at table nine; a process made more challenging than usual by the Frenchman, flamboyantly filleting a large bass on the same tiny service table for the two girls on table eight. There goes that bell again.

Vanilla panna cotta with raspberry jelly

Panna cotta alla vaniglia con gelatina ai lamponi

SERVES TWELVE PEOPLE

Ingredients

For the jelly:

360g raspberries (approx 4 each)

2 tsp gelatine powder

4 tbsps caster sugar

3 tbsp lemon juice

240ml cranberry juice

For the panna cotta:

5 leaves of gelatine

125g caster sugar

1 ltr whipping cream

1 tsp vanilla extract

25ml brandy

Method

To make the jelly:

1 Grease 12 moulds and place 4 raspberries in each.

2 Pour the lemon and cranberry juices into a pan and sprinkle with gelatine and sugar.

3 Simmer until the sugar and gelatine dissolve.

4 Divide the mixture between the moulds and place in the fridge for 1 hour, to set.

To make the panna cotta:

1 Place the cream, brandy and sugar into a pan. Soak the gelatine leaves in water or milk for 4–5 minutes, until soft.

2 Heat the cream, making sure that it does not boil. Place the gelatine into a 1½ ltr jug and then pour the warm cream over it. Mix them well together and leave to cool for 20–30 minutes.

3 Take the moulds out of the fridge and pour the mixture on top of the raspberry jelly. Put them back in the fridge and leave overnight. Make sure the cream mixture is cool before you pour it over the jelly.

4 Serve with a few fresh berries and mint leaves.

★ Tip: Remove the jellies from their moulds by dipping them in a bowl of hot water for 2–3 seconds and then turning them upside down. They should fall out onto your dessert plates.

"My wife Della is always attracted to the look of a dish, before the taste. She maintains this is one dessert that really does taste as good as it looks."

NELLO CIOTTI

Cannoli Siciliana

SERVES FOUR PEOPLE

Ingredients

For the snaps:

150g white flour

1 tbsp bitter cocoa

30g/2 level tbsp butter

1 egg

25g/2 level tbsp granulated sugar

60ml Marsala/red wine

12 steel tubes 3cm diameter (for moulds)

A pinch of salt

Oil, for frying

For the filling:

500g ricotta cheese

250g icing sugar

100g semi-sweet chocolate, diced into small pieces

50g pistachio nuts, chopped

A pinch of cinnamon

Candied orange peel

80g candied pumpkin

Method

1 Heap the flour on a pastry board and carefully work in the egg, butter, sugar, the cocoa (dissolved in Marsala or red wine) and a pinch of salt. When you have made a smooth dough, leave it to rest for about an hour. Roll it out in a thin sheet with a rolling pin and cut into 4 inch squares or use a pasta machine.

2 Roll each one diagonally around a steel tube. Press the edges together carefully with a dampened finger.

3 Deep fry until golden brown and leave to cool.

4 Meanwhile, work the ricotta with the icing sugar and cinnamon. Mix well with a wooden spoon, adding a few drops of milk if required. This cream should be smooth and rather thick.

5 Add the diced chocolate and the candied pumpkin then carefully remove the tubes and fill the cannoli with a teaspoon.

6 Garnish each of the cannoli with pieces of candied orange peel at either end. Partly dredge the cannoli with icing sugar.

"I love those old mob films where the New York Godfather sends the hit man out on a 'job', telling him to pick up a box of cannoli on the way back. For Sicilians, cannoli is a very traditional part of everyday life and a real reminder of home. Eat them with your hands and don't be shy about licking your fingers!"

NELLO CIOTTI

Caramelised Limoncello tart with salsa rossa

Torta al Limoncello con salsa rossa

SERVES TEN TO TWELVE PEOPLE

Ingredients

For the pastry:

200g flour

100g margarine

A little water

For the filling:

Juice of 2 lemons

125g caster sugar

6 eggs

500ml Guernsey double cream

75ml of Limoncello – at least!

Salsa rossa (red sauce – see page 116)

Method

1 Rub the flour and margarine together until they look like breadcrumbs, add a few drops of water and mix well until it becomes a firm dough. Leave to rest in the fridge for 30 minutes.

2 Roll the pastry, place into a 10 inch flan dish and blind bake in a medium oven (180°C) for 10 minutes.

3 Mix the eggs with the sugar until pale and then add the cream, lemon juice and Limoncello, mixing it all together well. Pour the finished mixture into the pastry case and bake for 50–60 minutes or until just set. Take out and leave to cool. Cut into portions, sprinkle with caster sugar and caramelise with a catering blowtorch or under a hot grill.

4 Serve with salsa rossa on the side.

"Limoncello is a popular drink with young Italians and is now fairly easy to get hold of outside Italy. We have our own special supply, which is made to a top secret recipe. Well, we can't give all our secrets away!"

RIVELINO RODRIGUES, SOUS CHEF

Zabaglione al Marsala

SERVES FOUR PEOPLE

Ingredients

4 egg yolks

3 tbsp Marsala wine

4 tbsp white wine

5 tsp caster sugar

8 sponge fingers or Cantuccini biscuits

Method

(You will need your best balloon whisk for this recipe.)

1 Half fill a pan of water and bring it to a simmer.
2 Put all the ingredients in a round-bottomed, stainless steel bowl that fits on top of the simmering pan of water, but without touching the surface.
3 Whisk the mixture by hand, slowly at first but then faster and continuously for 4–5 minutes, until it has doubled in size. Be careful: cook for long enough to ensure that the egg yolks are cooked; go on for too long and you risk ending up with something resembling alcoholic scrambled egg!
4 Pour into glass dishes and serve immediately with sponge fingers or Cantuccini biscuits.

★ Tip: For something a little different, drop some chopped fruit into the bottom of the glass dish first. Fresh strawberries or raspberries, or sliced, dried apricots all work well with this recipe.

"We recently brought back zabaglione, as part of a Sicilian menu month. It proved so popular that we had to keep it on."
TIM VIDAMOUR

Baked peaches and mascarpone cheese

Pesche al forno con mascarpone

SERVES FOUR PEOPLE

Ingredients

4–8 medium to large peaches depending on the size

250g mascarpone cheese

2 tbsp caster sugar

1 tsp ground cinnamon

2 vanilla pods

8 Amaretti biscuits

A pinch of ground nutmeg

1 tbsp demerara sugar

Method

1 Preheat the oven to 180°C. Cut the peaches in half and remove the stones. Place the peach halves on a grill tray with the flat side upwards.

2 Split the vanilla pods lengthways, scrape the seeds out with the tip of a knife and mix them together with the caster sugar, cinnamon and nutmeg. Sprinkle the mixture over the peaches and place in the pre-heated oven for 15–20 minutes.

3 Meanwhile, crush or blend the Amaretti biscuits and mix them with the demerara sugar.

4 Take the peaches out of the oven; place a teaspoon of mascarpone cheese into each cavity, sprinkle with the Amaretti biscuit mix and place under a medium to high grill, to brown.

5 Serve the peaches together on one big plate in the middle of the table and invite your guests to help themselves, Italian style. But make sure that you stress there are only 2 each!

"This is a lovely, easy summer dessert and typically Italian. My sister Angela grows beautiful peaches in the hills outside Rome. Try to get large peaches if you can, which split open easily. Don't worry about leftovers: they are delicious eaten cold the next day."

NELLO CIOTTI

A DAY IN THE LIFE ... 10.10 p.m.

The head hostess looks up from the bill spike and notices the time. ten minutes late.

'Eh, Maria's just called!' she shouts to the headwaiter, who grins and turns the sign on the door. Maria, who returned home to Portugal last year, was always a closing time stickler.

That's it: no more changes or chances. The restaurant is full, the spidery table plan history. The dining room is buzzing, contented and relaxed. Listen carefully and you'll hear the whole building breathing out.

Three tall, slim, tough-looking men are eating and drinking for six on a table for two. They joke quietly in an unintelligible tongue. The eldest, elegantly bald, catches the proprietor's eye, signalling for more red wine.

A third Barollo? Certainly. He returns with a bottle and the inevitable question.

'Where are you gentlemen from?'

Brows furrow and a hurried sketch map takes shape on a doyley. The Slovak waiter joins the huddle, dirty plates in both hands.

'Ah, Oo-cry-een!' he announces.

Nods, smiles, pride and amazement. They are delivering a Guernsey yacht to Odessa, in the Ukraine. It's their first, and probably last, night in Guernsey but they are doing it with panache – and symmetry; the port of Odessa was built from the finest Guernsey granite. The proprietor bids them safe passage and offers Da Nello's own Limoncello liqueur, iced and on the house.

The courtyard lights dim.

'Tre, due, uno... happy birthday to you, happy birthday...' The impromptu staff a capella envelops the table while the restaurant manager places a sparkling white roman candle on a plate in front of a bashful lady. The rest of the table struggles with cameras while the whole room joins in the singing. Flashbulbs light up the courtyard walls and the proprietor arrives bearing a long tiramisu birthday cake, a birthday kiss and a knife.

'Alright, which one of you did this?' The lady feels tricked and elated, all at the same time.

The restaurant manager leans past the barmaid and over the glass washing machine, catching a face-full of steam. His finger reaches past a wall of scrappy memos into the dark recess under the stairs, home to battered ledgers, sellotape, torches and the sound system. Two clicks and the Italian tenor is buried under the rumble of RL Burnside's blues guitar. Now it's the weekend. The phone rings once: 'Kitchen; five cold beers. Thanks.'

'I can't pretend any longer...' The proprietor hands a red rose to the tall, bemused brunette with a flourish.

The giggles grow as he wantonly woos his way through the party of girls, dispensing flowers and cringe-making couplets. The headwaiter has heard them all before but can't help smiling as he holds open the door.

Goodnight ladies. He follows them out with the Frenchman to retrieve the heavy window boxes of flowers. Outside, Le Pollet is jammed with taxis inching their way past revellers, hitting the night-clubs.

The sauces and pasta
I sughi e le paste

Complicated sauces are few and far between in Italy, where cooks prefer to let fresh, good quality ingredients speak for themselves. The Da Nello menu is no different, relying on these few basics.

Fish stock

(makes 1½ – 2 ltr)
see Fish Soup

INGREDIENTS

1kg of bones from a large brill or turbot
1 onion, chopped
2 carrots, chopped
2 celery stalks, chopped
6 black peppercorns
2 bay leaves
a few parsley stalks
2½ ltr of water

METHOD

Put all ingredients into a pan with the water and bring to the boil, skimming off any scum. Reduce the heat until it is simmering and leave it like this for 15 minutes. Strain and leave to cool. You can make this the day before and store it in the fridge, when cold.

Béchamel sauce

(makes 250ml approx)

see Lobster linguine, Crab Thermidor

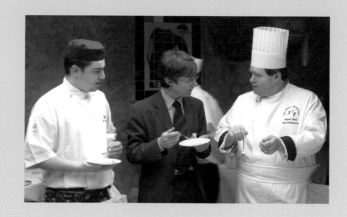

INGREDIENTS

250ml milk

20g Guernsey butter

20g plain flour

Salt and white pepper

Freshly ground nutmeg

METHOD

To make the béchamel sauce, melt 20g of butter slowly in a pan, so that it does not brown. Remove from the heat, add the flour, stir with a wooden spoon to create a roux and set to one side.

Bring the milk almost to the boil, add the milk to the roux, whisk continuously and turn the heat down low. Simmer this for 8–10 minutes, to cook the flour.

Season with salt, pepper and nutmeg (one pinch of each) and pour into a container to cool.

Thermidor sauce

(makes 250ml approx)

see Lobster linguine, Crab Thermidor

This can be made the day before

INGREDIENTS

250ml béchamel sauce

2 shallots, finely chopped

25ml dry white wine

20g Guernsey butter

25ml brandy

100g grated Gruyere cheese

1 tsp English mustard

A pinch of Cayenne pepper

METHOD

To make the Thermidor sauce, melt 20g of butter and sauté the shallots in a pan, until light brown (6–8 minutes). Add the brandy and white wine and simmer, tilting gently to set the mixture alight (flambé sounds better!). The flame will die away after 5 or 6 seconds. This is the time to add the béchamel sauce, mustard, Cayenne pepper and cream.

Bring to a simmer, add 100g of the grated Gruyere cheese and keep stirring. Reduce the mixture like this until you have a rich, light yellow, silky sauce.

Salsa Napolitana

(Napoli Sauce – makes 300ml approx)

see Lobster linguine, Bass Livornese

INGREDIENTS

50ml olive oil

1 shallot, finely chopped

400g tomatoes, skinned, de-seeded and chopped if using fresh (chopped, tinned, Italian plum tomatoes also work better)

1 clove of garlic, finely chopped

2 basil leaves, shredded

A pinch of caster sugar

Salt and pepper, to taste

METHOD

Gently sauté the onions in the oil until soft (5–6 minutes approx). Combine all the other ingredients, bring to a simmer and cook for 30 minutes, checking that it does not reduce too much (add a little water if needed). Liquidise in blender or food mixer.

Garlic butter

see Medallions of beef Barolo

This can also be used for many other dishes. Although it's not difficult to make, it involves quite a lot of work so it pays to make more than you need and keep some for other times.

INGREDIENTS

250g of soft Guernsey butter
1 onion, roughly chopped
6 cloves of garlic
2 tpsp of continental parsley
2 tbsp of brandy
1 tbsp of Lea & Perrin sauce
½ glass of Barolo, or any other 'meaty' Italian red wine. I like a nice Barolo Cordana, which is perfect for both the garlic butter and the sauce. The rest slips down rather nicely with the meal.
Juice of 1 lemon

METHOD

To make the garlic butter, place the onion, garlic and parsley into a blender and whizz until fine. Place the mixture in a bowl and add ½ a glass of red wine, lemon juice and Lea & Perrin sauce and brandy. Mix together and leave it to marinade for one hour.

Put the butter in the blender with the marinade and blend together. Take it out and use what you need. The rest will keep well in the fridge for 3–4 days, or for several months in the freezer.

Demi glace

(makes 1 ltr approx)

see Medallions of beef Barolo, Calves liver with whisky and pepper sauce,

Demi glace needs to simmer for several hours, so you may wish to make it a few days before you need it.

INGREDIENTS

900g beef bones

2 ltr water

100g carrot, chopped

50g onion, chopped

50g celery, chopped

200g tomatoes, chopped

50g butter

50g flour

2 cloves of garlic

2 sprigs of parsley

2 sprigs of thyme

2 sprigs of oregano

1 bay leaf

METHOD

Brown the bones in a hot oven in a roasting tray, together with the vegetables, for 20–30 minutes.

Place the bones and vegetables in a large pan and cover with cold water. Bring to a simmer and add the herbs and garlic. Simmer for 2–3 hours, skimming the fat off the top with a ladle.

Strain the stock into a clean pan and keep simmering.

Mix the butter and flour (known as beurre manié – meaning 'kneaded butter'), whisk into the sauce and simmer for 10 minutes.

Season with salt and pepper.

Red onion and Chianti sauce

see Rack of venison with red onion and Chianti sauce

INGREDIENTS

1ltr Chianti or other good red wine
2 red onions, thinly sliced into half
moons
1 tsp of chopped garlic
1 tbsp Dijon mustard
1 tbsp brown sugar
100ml balsamic vinegar
200ml demi glace

METHOD

Sweat off the onions and garlic in a little olive oil, until soft. Add the balsamic vinegar and sugar and reduce into a syrup. Add the mustard and Chianti and bring to the boil. Reduce, by half and simmer for 10-15 minutes or until it becomes a smooth, creamy sauce. Season with salt and pepper.

Béarnaise sauce

see Tagliata of Guernsey beef
Serves two people

INGREDIENTS

2 egg yolks
5g chopped shallots
3x crushed peppercorns
5g tarragon, leaves separated from the
stalks
1 tbsp white wine vinegar
100g Guernsey butter, melted

METHOD

Lay the tarragon stalks, shallots, peppercorns and vinegar in a pan and reduce to one third. Add 1 tablespoon of cold water, strain and allow to cool.

Whisk in the egg yolks, return to a gentle heat and, whisking continuously, cook to a sabayon (it should have the consistency of double cream).

Remove from the heat and gradually whisk in the warm, melted butter until thoroughly combined.

Season to taste, with salt and black pepper. Chop the tarragon leaves and add them to the sauce. Serve immediately.

Pesto Sauce

see Veal cutlet with thyme and lemon pesto

INGREDIENTS

4 small bunches of fresh basil leaves
2 garlic cloves
1 tbsp of pine nuts, lightly toasted (3–4 minutes in a hot oven)
2 tbsp of grated Parmesan cheese
Extra virgin olive oil
Salt

METHOD

Blend the basil, garlic, pine nuts and a pinch of salt in a food processor, until it forms a smooth paste.

Place in a bowl and mix in the Parmesan and enough olive oil to cover the pesto.

This sauce can be kept for 1–2 weeks in the fridge, in a jar, which means that it can be prepared well in advance.

Salsa rossa

see Caramelised Limoncello tart with salsa rossa

INGREDIENTS

200g raspberries
100g icing sugar
Juice of a lemon (or you could use the equivalent amount of peach, strawberry or mango juice)

METHOD

Place the raspberries and icing sugar into a bowl and mix. Cover with cling film and place in the fridge for 1 hour.

Liquidise in a blender or food mixer, pass through a fine sieve and add a little lemon juice, to taste.

PASTA

What every Italian girl learns from her mother:

Dried pasta

There is absolutely no shame in using pre-packaged pasta; without it, Italians would never get to Mass, drink espresso, build Ferraris or win the World Cup. Indeed, there are many popular dishes that would simply not work with fresh pasta, e.g spaghetti napoletana, spaghtetti aglio, olio e peperoncino, penne amatriciana etc.

Dried pasta is best for anything that should be eaten *al dente*, e.g. spaghetti, rigatoni, penne, bucatini etc. Always cook according to the instructions on the packaging – certainly never more. Use 1ltr of water for every 100g of pasta, plus 10g of salt. Always ensure that the water is boiling before putting the pasta in. Stir well whilst cooking and finish by draining thoroughly.

Tip: When cooking pasta – especially long varieties (spaghetti, vermicelli, fettucine etc) – it helps to add a tbsp of oil in the boiling water, to stop the pasta from sticking together.

Fresh pasta

Fresh pasta is usually made with eggs instead of water and lends itself to dishes that are baked in the oven, e.g. lasagne, cannelloni and, of course, the famous fettuccine and linguine.

Use 1ltr of water for every 100g of fresh pasta, plus 10g of salt. Always ensure that the water is boiling before putting the pasta in. As soon as fresh pasta floats to the surface it should be stirred gently for 1–2 minutes. It is then ready. Drain well and serve with your favourite sauce.

A DAY IN THE LIFE ... 12.45 a.m.

'Thank you, good night. Have a good weekend. Thank you.'

The headwaiter helps the 50th birthday party on with their coats as they file through the front door. The last man smiles guiltily and grabs a fistful of mints from the glass dish on the counter.

'Help yourself, sir. That's what they're for. Bye bye! Thank you!'

Gone. It's done.

The restaurant manager scans the wine racks like a conductor, silently noting each gap with a flick of his pen. He jots the totals on his clipboard then starts the process of faxing each column to the respective supplier. Not all deliver on a Saturday, so he'll collect some orders in the van on his way in tomorrow. Which is, of course, today.

There's laughter coming from the saletta. Lots of it. The reckless, half-exhausted, half-hysterical variety. A dark Portuguese waitress is laughing so much that she has had to sit down. Her petite colleague is trying and failing to help the big Slovak to join two big tables together with an extension leaf. He finally hoists the heavy board above his head.

'Funny, huh? Quicker I do myself!'

The Frenchman sips coke and offers insincere encouragement. The top two rooms must be completely reconfigured in time for Saturday night's circus, when a retirement party and a visiting cricket team are topping the bill. Meanwhile, the place is littered with spare chairs, ice buckets, coffee cups and dirty laundry. The restaurant manager arrives to chivvy them up.

The head hostess shakes her head as she puts the final lost item on the bar. Four cameras in one night; that might even be a record, plus the usual crop of umbrellas, birthday presents and purses. Mind you, nothing can beat that set of false teeth that turned up under table ten. The phone will start ringing in the morning and it will all find its way home.

The front door suddenly bursts open and a man in a grubby woolly hat lurches through, inching carefully towards the bar like a tightrope walker.

There's a long pause as he blinks slowly and prepares to speak.

'.....Shigarettes?'

It's the same, slurred, question he asks every time he staggers in. He could almost qualify as a regular customer.

'I'm sorry, I told you last time. We don't sell them. Try down the road. Goodnight, yes, thank you.'

He looks like he might turn nasty but smiles instead, gives a shaky wave and mouths a silent riposte. The head hostess rolls her eyes, crosses the bar and ushers him firmly out the door. No rose for him tonight.

Darkness descends as the restaurant manager runs his hand over the banks of light switches. Music off, back doors locked. The headwaiter ties the last black sack of empty bottles and heaves them out to the side door. The Slovak resumes his mobile Internet demonstration to the Frenchman, who is slipping on a leather jacket. They're off clubbing. Well, it is Friday after all. The restaurant manager shakes his head, locks up and walks home alone.

ACKNOWLEDGEMENTS

Of course food is important, but restaurants are all about personalities. We've met, fed and worked with many good people and to mention them all would fill several books, but those deserving special thanks are (in no particular order):

My wife Della, for putting up with a lifetime of late nights; my late in-laws Fred and Doris Brehaut, for all their support and encouragement; the late Cyril Herpe, No.46's previous owner, for giving so much help just when we needed it; the two Richards at Sommelier Wine Co; David Rondell, the free-thinking designer; The Milton Produce team, for 28 year's worth of wonderful veg; David Thompson, the tireless and resourceful builder; Seafresh Limited; Monty Lucas, the last fish trader in the market; Phoenix Foods Ltd; Mr & Mrs Douglas Chisholm, for teaching me the benefits of being British (including *The Daily Telegraph*); Caterquipe Ltd; Mr Richard Cann, for schooling a young Italian in the art of diplomacy; Hotel & Commercial Laundries Ltd; Dave the butcher; local historian John McCormack; Frank Hallam, for superb scallops; Mr & Mrs Joseph Fattorini; Carefree Plants; Mercury Distribution Guernsey Ltd; Mr Peter Finlinson, for always 'telling it how it is'; Wine & Beer Importers (Gsy) Ltd; French Accents; Ray and Jocelyn Watts at Meadow Croft Farm; PVS 94 and Bella Delicatessen; Mr Duncan Spence for editorial advice; Nick Després and Tim Feak for additional photography, plus a big fat *grazie* to all our regular customers and everyone who has helped us to get this far.

Recipes – Tim Vidamour and Nello Ciotti

Text – Marco Ciotti

Design – Mike Brain Graphic Design Limited

Concept, photography and production – Chris Andrews Publications